Tl
Great Siege
of
Bedford Castle

June 20th-August 14th, 1224

This edition prod ced by
PAUL HOOLEY & ASSOCIATES
29 Elstow Road · Kempston · Bedford MK42 8HD
June 1985

Original edition produced by
Bedfordshire Times Publishing Co. Ltd.
June 1906

For further information on the Town and Castle during this period, I recommend David and Evelyn Baker's recently produced *Beginnings of Bedford* published by the Planning Department of Bedfordshire County Council.

Foreword to 1985 Reproduction

I am persuaded for two particular reasons to reproduce this account of one of the great moments in our local history, which was of such national and international importance.

Firstly, and simply, to ensure a continuing availability of details of the event, painstakingly recorded by contemporary chroniclers, including the gifted Matthew Paris of St. Albans, and so well presented in the original version of this publication.

The second reason is the result of a series of recent coincidences.

In May of this year the North Bedfordshire Borough Council's Amenities Committee, of which I have the honour to be chairman, completed the move of Bedford Museum from The Embankment to newly renovated Bennetts Works, and began demolishing the old buildings standing on the former castle site as part of a continuing policy of enhancing the river frontage.

Returning the area to public open space, and making the castle mound an accessible and prominent feature, created a renewed interest in the history of the site.

I was approached by several people requesting information on the subject, including a friend who had lived in the Town for over 70 years and who now expressed annoyance at the lack of available details.

Within 24 hours of acknowledging my friends comments, and quite by chance, a copy of the account now reproduced here came into my possession. Published by Bedfordshire Times in June 1906, it is a valuable compilation of the records of the annalists of the time, and I am most grateful to Bedford County Press for allowing me to reproduce the work in its entirety.

Taking account of inflation during the intervening years, today's cover price compares favourably with the one shilling Bedfordshire Times charged in 1906.

The re-publication date of Thursday, June 20th, 1985 corresponds to the day, date and month when at Bedford in the year of 1224, and at the age of 16 years, Henry III, King of England began his assault on Bedford Castle.

THE KEEP AND MOUND OF BEDFORD CASTLE.

From the drawing in the MS of the 'Chronica Majora' of Matthew Paris, in the Library of Corpus Christi College,

THE GREAT SIEGE OF BEDFORD CASTLE.

A Chapter of Local History,
compiled from Original
and Contemporary Records.

By A. R. GODDARD, B.A.

Illustrated by facsimiles
of drawings from the
MS of Matthew Paris.

PRINTED AND PUBLISHED BY THE BEDS. TIMES PUBLISHING CO. LTD.,
MILL STREET AND HOWARD STREET, BEDFORD.

JUNE, 1906.

This Study is an enlargement of a Lecture delivered before the Bedford Arts Club and the Bedford Fröebel Society. The thanks of the writer are due to Mr. C. W. Moule, the Librarian of Corpus Christi College, Cambridge, and to the College Authorities, for permission to obtain photographs of the drawings in the Matthew Paris MS in their Library. Also to Mr. W. H. St. John Hope for valuable comments on the proof sheets; and to Mr. C. Gore Chambers for help with the technicalities of the Close Rolls.

THE GREAT SIEGE OF BEDFORD CASTLE.

SYNOPSIS.

Introductory.

Need of one of the old garrison to explain the site as it now is. The national and international import of the siege. The vividness of the story.

1. Concerning the Personages involved.

Henry III, the boy King. Hubert de Burgh. Henry de Braibroc and his wife. The Earl of Chester. William de Beauchamp. Fawkes de Breauté and his wife. William de Breauté. Minor characters.

2. Concerning the nature of the Castle.

Its reputed founder. Uncertainty of the exact date. At first only earthwork and stockade. Gradual substitution of stone for timber. Description in 1138. Besieged by Stephen. The Bridge. The town and its churches in 1224.

3. Concerning Annalists and Records.

The Prior of Dunstable. The scribe of St. Albans. The Abbot of Coggeshall. The King's Records; the Close and Patent Rolls. The contemporary correspondence.

4. Concerning the troubles of the times.

The state of affairs after the death of John. The French intrusion. Its end. Smouldering disaffection. The barons and the royal castles. Need of having loyal castellans in charge of them. The angry meeting at Waltham. Christmas of 1223. The King and his party at Northampton. The " Schismatics " at Leicester. Submission of the rebels. An end to land-stealing. The King returns to Northampton. Bad news from Dunstable.

5. Concerning the act which led to the siege.

The King's Justices at Dunstable. Fawkes de Breauté's conviction and penalty. The raid on the Justices and capture of De Braibroc. His imprisonment in Bedford Castle. How the King received the news.

6. Concerning the preparations for the siege.

The King's prompt march on Bedford. His orders for munitions of war. Particulars in the Close Rolls. Preparations to resist the Royal forces. The churches destroyed. Fawkes de Breauté not in the Castle. Where he was, and what he was doing. His sympathizers.

7. Concerning the Siege Artillery.

The great concourse with the King. Demand for the surrender of the Castle. Defiance of the garrison. Their excommunication. The siege engines and where placed. Mangonells, Balistæ, Petrary, and how they were worked.

8. Concerning the assaults.

Capture of the Barbican. Watchers in St. Mary's tower. Assault on the outer bailey and spoil taken. The miners under the 'cat.' The inner bailey taken. The rashness of the Dunstable men. The "beffrois." Losses on the King's side. The miners attack the mound and keep. Breach effected. The garrison strike their flag. How we know the keep was round and not square. Release of the captives. Fate of the garrison. De Breauté's wife and her action when released. The King's vow and how kept. Current lampoon.

9. Concerning the after-fortunes of Fawkes de Breauté.

Contemporary letters from two of his friends, the Earl of Chester and Llewelyn. Safe conduct for Fawkes to Bedford. He sees his friends on the gibbet. St. Alban's stone. De Breauté exiled. His appeal to the Pope. The Pope interferes, but too late. De Breauté's death, The judgment of Paris. The King claims money deposited by De Breauté.

10. Concerning the destruction of the Castle.

The orders for its demolition. Only a part to be given back to its former owner. His resistance to the King's instruction. Contemporary correspondence. Reduction of the mound. Position of the "old tower" and inner bailey. Distribution of the stone from the ruins. Slight traces of the works to-day. Only the mound in part remains. Its long life as a bowling green.

AUTHORITIES.

	Abbreviations in References.
ANNALES MONASTICI, Vol. III.—Dunstable Chronicle.	Duns. Chron.
RALF OF COGGESHALL.—Chronicon Anglicanum.	Cog. Chron.
MATTHEW PARIS.—Historia Anglorum, Vol. II.	M. Paris. H. A.
DITTO. Chronica Majora, Vol. III.	M. Paris. C. M.
CHRONICLES OF THE REIGN OF STEPHEN, &c., Vol. II.—Gesta Stephani.	Gest. Steph.
ROYAL AND HISTORICAL LETTERS, HENRY III. Vol. I. (The six preceding belong to the Rolls Series).	Royal Letters.
CLOSE ROLLS, DUFFUS HARDY, Vol. I. fol. 1833.	Close Rolls.
CALENDAR OF PATENT ROLLS, HENRY III. 1901.	Patent Roll.
J. H. ROUND.—Article 'The Castles of the Conquest,' in Archæologia, Vol. LVIII. 1902.	Round. Archæol.
G. T. CLARK.—Mediæval Military Architecture, Vol. I. 1884.	Clark. Med. Mil. Arch.
VIOLLET LE DUC.—Military Architecture, Macdermott's Translation, 1879.	Viollet le Duc.
PAYNE-GALLWEY.—The Crossbow, 1903.	
HURST.—Article 'Historical Notice of Bedford Castle.' Beds. Arch. Society's Trans., Vol. I., 1850-1.	Hurst.
WYATT.—Article 'Bedford after the Saxon Period.' Ditto. Ditto. Vol. IX., 1867-8.	Wyatt.
CARY ELWES.—Article 'Bedford Castle.' Ditto. Ditto. Vol. XII., 1873-4.	Elwes.
HARTSHORNE.—Bedford Castle, 1861.	
DICTIONARY OF NATIONAL BIOGRAPHY.	Dict. Nat. Biog.
NOTES BY MR. W. H. ST. JOHN HOPE.	W. H. St. J. H

THE ILLUSTRATIONS.

The three Matthew Paris drawings have not been reproduced before, and are the exact size of the originals. Architectural detail must not be taken as accurate. The photographs are by Mason and Basébé of Cambridge.

I. Frontispiece.

Drawing of the Mound and circular Keep of Bedford Castle. The outer wall round the top of the mound is the 'chemise.' The royal banner flies over the keep; de Breauté's over the gibbet. The wave-like drawing of the mound indicates its rise above the level ground. The corner of the vellum page has been cut off.

II. Plan of the present Environs of the Castle site.

Adapted from the 25 in. Ordnance Map.

III. The great stone descending on Fawkes de Breauté at St. Albans.

In the text occurs the reference to his penance.

IV. The death of Fawkes de Breauté at St. Ciriac. Recorded on the 4th line.

The drawing shows a demon directing the poisoned fish into his mouth. His shield is reversed on the left of the column. The top of the page has been cut in re-binding.

The Great Siege of Bedford Castle.

It does not often occur to us to associate with the touch of vanished hands or the sound of stilled voices the fragments of time-worn masonry or heaps of mounded earth which have come down to us from other and earlier days. Such things seem rather the result of geological process, giving feature to our dwelling places and alignment to our ways; and it is hard to realise that they are product of the travail of the men and women who went before us.

When our learned societies come to establish psychic communication with our departed forbears on a somewhat firmer footing than at present, we should be able to receive much light that we now lack as to the historic remains which so greatly interest us. If only, for instance, we could ring up from the shades William de Breauté, brother of the famous Fawkes, and persuade him to lead us round the Bedford castle precincts, how breathlessly should we hang upon his ghostly comment. It might puzzle him to make his way about now-a-days, but he would still find some of the old familiar landmarks remaining, which were so constantly in his eye, seven hundred years ago. We can hear him murmur—"Here stood our old castle gate, with its barbican fronting St. Paul's, and overlooking the bridge. Here ran our outer walls, ramparts, and ditches. Here, in line with the Inner Bailey walls, on the side nearest St. Paul's, was the

Ancient Tower. There is the very mound, our 'mota,' at least the stump of it, on which stood our circular keep. There flows the old Ouse, much where it did when our enemies pounded us across it with their siege engines. There are the two church towers, out of our range—St. Peter's in the Fields to the north, and St. Mary's on the south, from which the townspeople used to watch the siege. And there, alas! between mound and river, is the exact site of the gibbet of tree trunks on which my earthly pilgrimage was ended."

The banks of Ouse, placid enough now, and the earthen root of the stronghold which once commanded them, have only a local and recreational interest for us to-day, but when Fawkes de Breauté was active hereabouts, the eyes of all the English nation were intent upon them, and the eyes of many in the great world without; of Louis VIII, King of France, of Pope Honorius III., not to mention Llewelyn ap Jorwerth, Llewelyn the Great, Prince of pugnacious Welshmen.

The drama here unfolding was one of both national and international moment. Like all dramas, it had its antecedent story, leading up to the later crisis, and final issue. It had its sympathetic and antipathetic characters. It had its women, with their everlasting intervention for weal or woe. It also had its dramatists, who wrote the business up for us; often, after their kind, colouring the facts to suit their own ideas.

And yet the characters in the drama were not play-actors. It was a very real and strenuous business, with no smell of the footlights about it, and innocent of the unities, or harmonies, or any artificial stage management. There is not much in it that sounds a lofty note to stir our minds to admiration. Greed, ambition, craft, violence, are there in abundance, with a certain constant element of animal courage, and plenty of blood-letting. Even such religious motives as appear belong to the type which turns sacred things into weapons of superior efficacy for the overthrow of enemies, the securing of desired ends, and the justification of unstinting revenge. It is, on the whole, a study of life on a low level, but yet, for all that, full of human interest, as a manifest and naked display of what men and women, high and low, really did, saw, and suffered, in the year 1224, on ground mostly well known to us. The one voice that has the ring of a big living soul behind it comes from over the Welsh mountains.

1. Concerning the Personages involved. 1

Chief amongst the persons concerned appears a lad of 16, *Henry III, King of England*, crowned seven years before, on the death of his father John. The factions of the previous reign were always on the smoulder, and often bursting into a blaze, but through all the reek of it, one underlying principle was gradually gaining the upper hand:—England for the English, and neither for French King, nor foreign adventurers; especially not for the emissaries or agents of Papal Rome. Henry was moving early into a premature manhood under pressure of hard responsibilities. The year before the siege, Pope Honorius had sent a bull declaring the boy of age, for Rome at that time was well content 2
to see a puppet on the English throne, who was like to be plastic under Papal fingers for the support of Roman exactions against the English church and people.

By the young King's side, director and faithful counsellor, stood *Hubert de Burgh*, his Justiciar. At the death of the Regent, William Marshall, in 1219, he became Henry's Bismarck, until, like him, he was dropped overboard in his old age, a pilot for whom his King had no further use. Hubert was a stout man of war and sturdy Englishman. We must not look to Shakespeare's King John to read his character. In John's time he had held Dover against France, and in 1217, Henry's first year,

---

1. For further detail see Dict. Nat. Biog. under the various names.
2. Duns. Chron. p. 82.

had won a great naval victory for England over an out-numbering French fleet off the coast of Kent.

A central figure in our drama is *Henry de Braibroc* who, because of the faithful performance of his duty as one of the King's justices at Dunstable, fell into serious trouble, of which we shall hear later. He, too, was a good soldier, and had successfully defended Montsorrel castle against the forces of John, and incidentally, against Fawkes de Breauté, who was one of the commanders of the besieging army. De Braibroc's lady, Christiana, daughter of Wiscard Ledet, plays a wifely part in securing relief for her husband in his hour of trouble.

Next, we have *Randulf de Blunaevill*, the Earl of Chester, a busy schemer amongst the disaffected barons. He gave the King and his Justiciar many anxious moments. Any who were restive under the growing power of the central government, such as William de Fortibus, the Earl of Albemarle, Llewelyn of Wales, Fawkes de Breauté, and others, found in Earl Ralph a wily backer, ever ready to hie them on—"Go it, good dogs!" and also adroitly able after each escapade to emerge himself, safe, if discredited. This man took no direct part in our siege, but he harboured the King's enemies, and did what he could to discount his successes.

One of the lesser men on the side of the King was the hereditary lord of Bedford castle, *William de Beauchamp*. He had cast in his lot with the Barons when they exacted the Great Charter from John in 1215, and he threw open his castle to entertain them as they were on their way to London. For this, he paid the price of eviction. A few months later, by John's instruction, Fawkes de Breauté turned him out, and received the castle as his reward. Naturally, William de Beauchamp rallied to the new King's side, when he saw the chance of coming by his own again.

Now comes into view the villain of our piece, the said *Fawkes de Breauté*, who pretty well fills the stage with his

strut, except, curiously enough, during the nine weeks' siege of his castle. Fine soldier, lucky adventurer, ruthless buccaneer, we cannot do better than introduce him in the words of the Coggeshall chronicler: "King John had a certain servant, faithful and daring, who was nick-named Falco, from the scythe with which he had slain a soldier on his father's land in Normandy; to whom he at first entrusted a ward on the Welsh marches, where, with his friends and fellows, he had ravaged and massacred; so that from the lowest estate he had quickly become famous, capable, and highly distinguished among
those serving the King." At the time of our drama, he is a 1
baron of the realm, sheriff of seven counties, castellan of many royal castles and baron of the Exchequer. He had an inordinate lust for other people's lands, and a vicious distaste for the religious. A few years before, he had harried the monks of Warden, and as soon as he was established in Bedford castle, he swept down on the abbey and town of St. Albans, nefariously slaying the abbot's cook, and exacting a ransom of 100 pounds of silver as the price of his departure. He seems to have had some sort of lurking idea that injured monastics possessed powers of retribution beyond his understanding, and so made amends of a minor sort in both cases. At St. Albans he bared his back to the rods of the brotherhood,
and then severally kissed each individual monk. But for all his 2
penance he still held on to the 100 pounds of silver. He therefore remained on the black books of the abbey, and Matthew Paris, its chronicler, does not fail to point out that St. Alban took especial care to make the score even.

Fawkes de Breauté's wife was Margaret, formerly widow of the son of William de Ripariis, or Redvers, and the good lady makes a startling appearance on the closing scene.

---

1. Cog. Chron. p. 204.
2. See Plate III. 4th line from bottom, "Osculans singulos monachos."

The brother of Fawkes, ***William Martel de Breauté***, closes our list of characters in chief. He held Bedford castle during the absence of Fawkes, and only visibly appears twice in the story. Once, quite suddenly, at Dunstable, and then at the end of his desperate defence, when he bids us farewell from a lofty eminence, after the manner of Haman.

Besides all these personages, there is the usual troop of secondary characters. A pope; the noble archbishop, Stephen Langton; a papal legate; many bishops and abbotts; barons of various degrees; Knights Templar; soldiers in harness, not forgetting a gallant contingent from Dunstable; miners, siege-carpenters, and monks of Newenham and Warden, who furnish material towards their enemy's discomfiture. Also the Welsh Prince, always glad of an opportunity to embarrass his hereditary foe, the English King.

Altogether, a very sufficient caste, drawn together by the hand of destiny, with tuckets, excursions, and alarums in abundance.

ii. Concerning the Nature of the Castle.

So much for the persons concerned, let us now turn to the chief scene.

Paganus, or Payne de Beauchamp, the second son of Hugo,
1 the Conqueror's man, was, to quote G. T. Clark, who follows others without naming authorities, "the reputed founder of the first Bedford castle." Although Hugo had received 20 manors and estates in the county from King William, besides many others in Buckinghamshire, he was never Lord of Bedford, neither does Domesday mention any castle. It follows that the story of Hereward's imprisonment in 1071, in the donjon here, is more than doubtful.

---

1. Clark. Med. Mil. Arch., I. p. 218.

The actual facts as to the foundation of the castle have not yet emerged from the early mists, but, as it must have been soon after the Conquest, we can form a fairly faithful idea as to its character. By the comparative study, during the last 20 years, of early Norman strongholds, many misconceptions have been dispelled, and some degree of certainty has taken the place of random guess-work. Mr. Round's summary in his "Castles of [1] the Conquest," puts the matter concisely, and Bedford was no exception. It must have been a "moated mound with its timber palisade, and its moated and palisaded court or courts." Just such a work, in fact, as we may now see on Totternhoe Knoll, or at Cainhoe and Meppershall. In these instances, if you supply the stockading, make good the crumbling ramparts, and deepen the ditches, you have the thing complete, and may compare it with the drawings in the Bayeaux tapestry for confirmation.

There is little doubt that the earliest state of Bedford castle was as follows, all of it the work of Norman times. First, the great motte, 'mota,' or mound of earth, crowned by a keep of timber stockade, with a huge fosse round about it, from which the earth mostly came. Part of both mound and ditch remain for us still to see. Next to it, with Newenham road for its eastern [2] limit, was an inner court, or bailey, with high enclosing rampart, also stockaded, and with deep outer ditch. Beyond this again, stretching to the river on the south, the High street on the west, and Ram lane on the north, was the outer bailey, also banked, moated, and stockaded. The chief entrance was probably on the west side, overlooking the main street of the town and the bridge, which then was very likely of timber.

As time went on, stone walls took the place of stockade, but gradually. There was good reason for some interval before the appearance of masonry, that the stuff of mound and ramparts

---

1. Round. Archæol. VIII. p. 334.
2. See Plate II.

II.

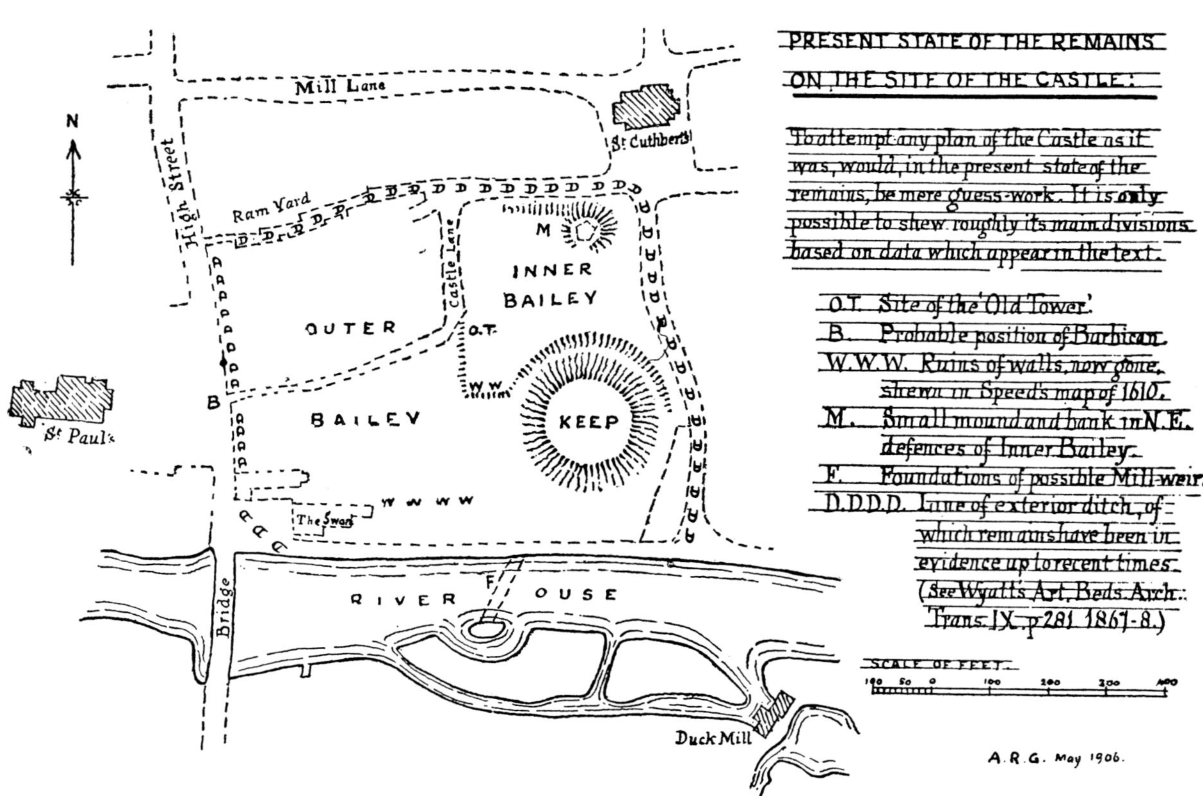

PRESENT STATE OF THE REMAINS
ON THE SITE OF THE CASTLE:
To attempt any plan of the Castle as it was, would, in the present state of the remains, be mere guess-work. It is only possible to shew roughly its main divisions based on data which appear in the text.
O.T. Site of the 'Old Tower.'
B. Probable position of Barbican.
W.W.W. Ruins of walls, now gone, shewn in Speed's map of 1610.
M. Small mound and bank in N.E. defences of Inner Bailey.
F. Foundations of possible Mill-weir.
D.D.D.D. Line of exterior ditch, of which remains have been in evidence up to recent times. (See Wyatt's Art, Beds Arch. Trans. IX. p 281 1867-8.)
SCALE OF FEET
100 50 0 100 200 300 400
A.R.G. May 1906.
N
Mill Lane
High Street
St Cuthbert's
St Paul's
Ram Yard
Castle Lane
INNER BAILEY
OUTER BAILEY
O.T.
M
W.W.
KEEP
B
W W W W
The Swan
Bridge
RIVER OUSE
F
Duck Mill

might settle into a compact mass before it was safe to top them with the weight of stone walling. The mound took longest to settle, and thus the stockaded keep might remain even after the ramparts were girt with stone walls. When this was done, it is
probable, that what is called by the Dunstable chronicler 'the 1
Ancient Tower,' was built somewhere on the western lines of the inner bailey. Finally, perhaps early in Stephen's reign, the stockaded keep on the mound made way for a circular stone keep of the 'shell' type.

A description of the castle at this stage is given us by the writer of the 'Gesta Stephani,' in dealing with the siege of 1138, when the place was held by Milo de Beauchamp against King
Stephen. Then the castle "was completely ramparted round 2
with an immense earthen bank and ditch, girt about with a wall, strong, and high, strengthened with a strong and unshakable keep, and filled with tough and unconquered men."

The place was not then taken by assault, for, after a five weeks' siege, during which the Royal headquarters were at Goldington, Milo and his men were allowed to march out on honourable terms. It was at the Christmas-tide of a very rainy winter, and the rising waters must have added to the difficulties of the besiegers.

Fifty years later, we come upon the first mention of a bridge
in the Pipe Roll of 34 Henry II. (1187-8), when we learn that 3
the Sheriff had spent £4 6s. 0d. "in the works of the bridge of the castle of Bedeford, and of the postern towards the water." Does this refer to the main bridge, or to a special way across the river for the castle alone? Probably the latter, for the reference to the postern gate suggests it, and the line of foundations under water which led to the island on the south, from the bank near

1. Duns. Chron. p. 86.
2. Gest. Steph. p. 31.
3. Elwes, Beds. Arch, Trans., XII. p. 249.

1 the mound, may have been its sub-structure. A drawbridge from the island would secure its southern approach. This
2 masonry was removed to be used in building the Howard Chapel in 1774, but its course is sometimes outlined by the water-weeds in summer, and may be seen when the river is low.

Such, then, was the stronghold, which in the year 1224 had come to be the most important feature of the Bedford of that day. War and worship claimed the chief structures in the town and suburbs. There were at least 5 churches rising above the house-tops, and the religious foundations of St. John's Hospital, Newenham, and Elstow priories. The smooth stream of the Ouse crawled sluggishly past, then as now, but more given to sudden invasion of the lower town and lands.

iii. Concerning Annalists and Records.

Here we must learn something of the writers and records from whom we hear what happened at the time of the great siege. The importance of the event is shown by the widespread
3 references in many of the old chronicles. In the scriptoria, or writing-studios, of our abbeys, scholarly monks were setting down in their annals, not merely the domestic details of monastic life, the succession of abbots and priors, the accidents, fires, and disturbances, but also the leading events in the world outside. They heard of these, often firsthand, from travelling strangers, royal or official visitors, or from such of their own people as might be more or less directly concerned.

---

1. Or it may have been a weir to raise the level of the water in the Castle Mill stream.

2. Hurst Ibid., I., p. 389.

3. "The carrels in the cloister were the only scriptoria." W. H. St. J. H. "In every window of the cloyster were three pews or carrels; where everyone of the old monks had his carrol, several by himself, to which, having dined, they did resort and there study their books. (Ancient Rites of Durham, p. 131). Parker's Glossary, I. p. 87.

We shall draw largely from three of these sources of history, inasmuch as being nearest to the scene of action, they are naturally fullest of detail. Twenty miles to the south of Bedford, the great priory of Dunstable had been founded by Henry I. about a century earlier. Twelve miles to the south-west of this, along the old Watling Street, was the more ancient abbey of St. Albans, established by a contemporary of Charlemagne, the Saxon King Offa, whose bones were raped from his mortuary chapel at Bedford by the invading waters of the Ouse. Forty-five miles again to the east, in Essex, Coggeshall abbey was in its prime, with new buildings rising up in finely-moulded red brick. In all three, chroniclers busied themselves in setting down the story of Falcasius de Breauté, how he flourished like the proverbial green bay, how he fell, and for his wickedness was rooted up. Let us give our historians reality by naming them.

The prior of Dunstable, from 1202 to his death in 1242, was 1
Richard de Morins, a well-known man in the Church far beyond his own nation. Before his work in the chronicle begins in 1210, earlier writers had drawn on Diceto, the entries only becoming original in 1201. As to the events of 1224, with which we are concerned, he could obtain the details direct from eye-witnesses.

Matthew Paris, at St. Albans, was an annalist of many 2
and varied gifts. He had the true historian's sense of proportion, and wrote a free and graphic style. He could draw and paint, as the marginal illustrations to his manuscripts show, and even work in gold and silver. He succeeded Roger of Wendover as Chief Scribe in the scriptorium of the abbey, and much of his work consisted of transcripts of his former master's entries, but with large extensions drawn from his own personal knowledge. His works, from which we obtain much vivid material, are the

1. Duns. Chron. Intro. and Dict. Nat. Biog.
2, M. Paris. H. A. & C. M. Intro, and Dict. Nat, Biog.

'Chronica Majora,' and 'Historia Anglorum.' At the time when de Breauté raided St. Albans, Matthew was a youth of 17½, and a novice of only six months' standing. He had, therefore, good reasons for following with interest that great rascal's after career.

1 *Ralf de Coggeshall* had been elected Abbot in 1207. He resigned from failing health in 1218, still staying on in the house, and working at his 'Chronicon Anglicanum.' He also was indebted to an earlier history, that of Ralph Niger, but from the entries of 1187, it is thought that we have the Abbot's original matter. Curiously enough, all extant MSS. end with his account of the Bedford siege.

Many other Chronicles have brief references to the business: so great a bruit throughout all England did it create, and so keenly did good Englishmen and good Christians watch for judgment to fall on this low-born sacrilegious French adventurer.

In all these monastic narratives there is an admixture of rumour and tradition, but there are other records of the time to which we may turn for definite particulars, confirmatory and corrective. Such are the carefully kept minutes of the Royal business and orders known as the Close and Patent Rolls, and a great body of State correspondence, lately collected and edited by Shirley, in a volume of the Rolls series, under the title, "Royal and Historical Letters."

These interesting letters had long been lost in the dusty masses of our national lumber. Prynne had noted and published some of them in 1672, and Bréquigny others in 1764. It was only in 1841 that Duffus Hardy came upon some of the long-lost
2 bundles, scheduling some 2,000 letters. Others have come to light since, and they now form a distinct department of our Public Records.

---

1. Cog. Chron. Intro. and Dict. Nat. Biog. "There is only strong presumptive evidence that Abbot Ralf was the Coggeshall chronicler." W. H. St. J. H.

2. Royal Letters. I. Intro,

From Shirley's volume we may cull 27 letters, many of them very long, concerning this business of Fawkes de Breauté, covering a period of 10 years. In them we have the very structure of history. There are letters, to or from, the King, Hubert de Burgh, Pope Honorius III. and his legate Pandulf, Stephen Langton, Fawkes de Breauté, William de Beauchamp, the Earl of Chester, Llewelyn, and others concerned. They throw a fuller light on the subject, which has not hitherto been available.

iv. Concerning the Troubles of the Times.

The ground thus cleared, we are free to watch the movement and action of the participants in due sequence.

The granting of the great Charter had been followed by the machinations of John to regain the upper hand, and by the entrance of a French Prince at the invitation of the resisting barons. John's death, after the disaster in the Wash, suddenly 1
changed the whole situation. The boy King, whose power for harm at nine years of age was small, became the rallying centre for all the best men in the land, headed at first by William Marshall, and later by Hubert de Burgh. The French escapade ended with the break up of the dissident allies at Lincoln. A strong central Government, with the boy King for figure-head, had become the chief necessity of the moment. The unruly barons, with their following, who had tasted the delights of mutiny, must not be allowed to become small kings, each fighting for his own hand, and ready to launch into new orgies of blood and faction. It soon became clear that it was of the utmost importance to secure the return of the King's many castles to the hands of the King's own men. As we have seen, Fawkes de Breauté was a great pluralist in castles. He had been John's right-hand man. Even of boy Henry, during the early years of

1. "In the Wellstream." W. H. St. J. H.

the reign, he had deserved well. His position, therefore, became somewhat dubious. He kept on terms with the King's party, but, in 1220, secretly aided an abortive attempt at revolt by William de Fortibus, Earl of Albemarle. In this year Pope
1 Honorius intervened with a bull supporting the King in his demand for the return of his castles.

Two years later, a dangerous pro-French outburst blazed up in London. Fawkes had little to hope for from Louis, and he strenuously worked with Hubert de Burgh to stamp it out. When the Justiciar shrank from executing the leaders, de Breauté promptly strung them up, regardless of tempting proffers of ransom.

In spite of all this the Justiciar did not slacken in his main policy. The castles must be given up. Fawkes was in no mind to have his own claws clipped. Signs of the friction appear in the Patent Roll for the autumn of 1223 and the following spring. Fawkes was stiffly enjoined that he should cause the castles of
2 Oxford, Hertford, Carisbrook, Christchurch, and Plympton to be handed over to castellans named by the King. When, therefore, in 1223, Llewellyn broke out again, he watched the movement with satisfaction, and soon after, with William de Fortibus, the Earl of Chester, and others, made a dash for the Tower of London; but the attempt was foiled. They next met the King in person at Waltham, the Archbishop acting as mediator, in hopes of reconciliation. The Dunstable Chronicle describes the interview. The malcontents demanded that the faithful Justiciar should be sent about his business. "Hubert de Burgh," they said, "is a waster of the King's treasure, and an oppressor of the people." Hubert answered them hotly, especially turning on Peter de Roches, Bishop of Winchester, a pro-French and pro-Rome maker of much mischief, and roundly called him "a traitor

1. Royal Letters, CIV. p. 121, also Appendix V. No. 9.
2. Ibid. Appendix II. Nos. 5, 11, 15, 21, 23, and 24.

to King and Kingdom, and the malicious cause of all the evils which had befallen, both in the last reign and the present." The Bishop, "pro malis mala refundens," giving back as good as he got, declared that if it cost him his last penny he would oust the Justiciar from place and power. Then, rushing from the midst with his confederates, he withdrew muttering. All this "coram
rege," in the King's very presence. A significant little prologue 1
to the subsequent drama.

Through all the raging of violent and headstrong men, the seasons, unresting, fulfil their cycle, and now the festival of Christ's birth was at hand. The King prepared to keep the feast at Northampton. The 'Scismatics,' as the Chronicle calls them, took themselves off to Leicester. The King entered Northampton, and with him "the Lord Archbishop of Canterbury, and so many bishops, earls and barons, and armed knights,
that neither in the days of his father, nor afterwards, was such a 2
festival kept in England."

This imposing show of force was too much for the 'Scismatici.' Five days later they came in, and after solemn admonition from the Archbishop, both they who were of their part, and they who were for the King, surrendered into his hands the wardship of their castles.

Thus ended that notable Christmastide, in jubilation for the King's friends, and confusion for his enemies.

Hubert de Burgh's next business was like to the last. Castles wrongfully held against the King; or lands filched from their rightful owners, were all of one. In the matter of land-grabbing, Fawkes de Breauté was a sinner of the front rank. Two years before, William Marshall, the younger, had complained by letter to the Justiciar that de Breauté had laid hands on certain of his lands in Bedfordshire. Even after the return of the castles,

1. Duns. Chron. p. 83.
2. Ibid. p. 84.

Hubert de Burgh hears again from the same quarter, seconded by William Longsword, Earl of Salisbury, almost in the same words, that John Marshall, kinsman of William, had sent Fawkes de Breauté letters of the lord King, demanding the return of a wood and lands at Norton, and that Fawkes had burst out, before his servant, calling John Marshall and all native-born Englishmen traitors, bidding the man be sure and repeat his exact words to his master; and that, though they sent him "30 pairs of letters," he
1 would not give up the lands, not he. Moreover, he had shut up John's bailiff in Northampton castle.

This was in the spring of 1224, and soon afterwards the King and his Council are again at Northampton, devising means to deal with a French invasion of Picardy. Whilst they deliberate
2 with their hands very full, there is a sudden interruption. The noble lady, Christiana, wife of Henry de Braibroc, has come in, post haste, with very bad news from Dunstable.

V. Concerning the Act which led to the Siege.

Here we change our scene to the little town which had sprung up about the monastic house of "the blessed Peter at Dunestapel." It is the octave of Pentecost, the 16th June, 1224. On that day, whilst the winds were whistling, after their wont, over the Five Knolls, there was an unusual concourse in the
3 streets. Three of the King's justices—"Itinerants," we call them, says Matthew Paris—had been holding their Court "de nova disseisina"; that is to right the wrongs of those whose lands had been unjustly disseised. Amongst them were 32 freemen of the Manor of Luton, who had been deprived, without judicial process, of certain tenements and rights in common pastures. The

1. Royal Letters, LIX. p. 71; CLII. p. 175; CXCVI. p. 220; CXCVII. p. 222.
2. Duns. Chron. p. 86, and M. Paris. H. A. II. p. 263.
3. M. Paris. Ibid.

offender was the said Falcasius de Breauté. The Court had
risen, and to the immense glee of everybody in the town, the big
jumper of claims had been compelled to disgorge. The crowd rush
about telling the story; with exaggerations, no doubt, so that
Matthew Paris says there were more than 30 convictions against 1
him; the Dunstable Chronicle 35; but the King, writing to Pope
Honorius, says 16. Moreover, for every conviction, Paris states
that a fine of £100 was inflicted.

Small wonder if the great church of the abbey rang that night with the triumphal Psalms of the brotherhood, or if the townsmen drank good luck to their three lordships of the King's Bench, Henry de Braibroc, Martin de Pateshulle, and Thomas de Milton. Meanwhile, the justices themselves, probably guests of the abbey, might well chuckle over their wine, stretching their limbs at leisure, after a good day's work, well done. If so, their complacency was brought to a speedy end. There is a sudden bustle without. A trusty servant comes in with anxious face, and tells the justices that the day's work is not done, not by any means done, for William de Breauté and his men are in full cry after their worships, galloping hard from Bedford castle; and that if they would preserve their worshipful skins in suitable soundness, it were well for them to make themselves very immediately scarce. The which they lost no time in doing.

"Now the justices," says Matthew Paris, "having timely warning, took themselves off, wherever their hasty rush chanced to
carry them." Apparently they scattered, but the wily de Breau-
téans lay in ambush, and "incaute fugiens," straight into their
arms, poor Henry de Braibroc ran. Losing the others, the
soldiers made sure of him, and handling him none too gently, shut
him up in the dungeon of Bedford castle keep. 2

---

1. M. Paris. H. A. p. 263; Duns. Chron. p. 90; Royal Letters. CXCIX. p. 225.
2. M. Paris. H. A. p. 263.

Such was the story that his wife Christiana, with many tears, laid before King and Council at Northampton. Their indignation was mighty, and their decision immediate. The French business can wait. They must deal with this insolent rebel at once, and vindicate the outraged law of King and Kingdom.

vi. Concerning the Preparations for the Siege.

From Northampton to Bedford is only 21 miles. The tidings
1 came in on June 16. By the 21st the King had transferred his headquarters here, and is sending out his mandates right and and left all over the country. Meanwhile, we may picture the flutter of the perturbed inhabitants.

The first thing to be done was to surround and blockade the brigand's den; then to press the siege hard and fast. Even when the royal forces had encompassed their enemy, there were great preparations to be made. The King, or rather his Justiciar, would be under no delusion as to the nature of the enterprise, and they drew upon the whole resources of the kingdom that they might make a final end of Falcasius and his ill-doings; such an end as should be a salutary warning to all who were inclined to withstand the royal authority.

2 The Close Rolls of that time are full of the business. In the entries appear the orders of the King, with the Royal attestation, often witnessed by Hubert de Burgh and others, in which, from all parts of the land he calls for men, money, supplies, and munitions of war. On the march to Bedford a halt had been made at Newport Pagnell for a day, and several of the orders date from there. In all appears the note of urgency. "Without delay,"

---

1. Close Rolls. p. 605.
2. Ibid.

" With all haste," " At sight of these letters," are frequent expressions used.

The sheriff of London is to send 2 or 3 waggons of cord and 20 slings, for mangonells and petraries; also targes and quarrells, as many as possible; ten good cables, with men of London City, well equipped; one Clerk for King's messenger; wine from the Tower, 30 dolia or casks; 200 pick-axes; tents for both King and Justiciar; and harness. Five or six smiths are to work day and night to make quarrells, which must be sent with all despatch. Also 200 lumps of wax, no doubt for waxing the cords of the engines.

The bailiffs of Cambridge and Northampton are to send good cords and cables, as many as possible; and, under safe conduct, ten white bull hides, or horse hides, or 12 tanned hides, to make slings for the petraries and mangonells. Also two pack-horses with men and all furnishings, and nails, and everything needed for the " targias inarmandas," which I take to be shields not yet covered.

The constable of Windsor is to send the master carpenter and his mates, with horses and tools. The King's treasurer is to send supplies of money from the royal Exchequer. The constable of the town and the sheriff of Northampton are to send wine. Ralph Gernon, of Corfe castle, is to send 12,000 one-foot, and 13,000 two-foot quarrels. Dr. Morris tells me this refers to the two sizes of cross-bows; those drawn by placing one foot in the stirrup, and those needing both feet.

My own extracts from the entries being incomplete, the items that follow are drawn from Mr. G. T. Clark's summary.

The King's mandates require men, money, arrears of scutage payments, iron, steel, and stône shot; quarrymen, masons, saddlers; almonds, spice, and ginger, from the Royal stillroom. Knights on castle guard at Lancaster are ordered up, even two men from the same service at Newcastle-on-Tyne. Greyhounds are wanted for the King's sport. The sheriff of Bedfordshire

must supply quarrymen and masons, with levers, hammers, mauls, and wedges, and all requisites for preparing stone shot for the engines. Miners are to come from St. Briavels, in the Forest of Dean, and charcoal with iron and steel from Gloucester. The
1 adjacent monks of Newenham are to supply much raw stone to be turned into shot.

Thus we gain glimpses of the fervour of preparation. The other side was equally busy. For some time past de Breauté had been strengthening himself against the evil day. Now that it was upon them, the few days between the Dunstable capture and the appearance of the avenging army would be full of work for the besiegers. There were cattle and stores to be collected over and above those already placed; the men of the garrison to be assigned to their posts; timber-screens and scaffolds to be reared on the wall tops; the artillery of defence to be finally prepared and proved; and the quarrells and stone shot to be apportioned ready to hand.

One act of military precaution made a bad impression on all who saw or heard of it. Two churches stood just outside the castle walls, St. Paul's on the west, and St. Cuthbert's at the north-east angle. Their towers must have overlooked the castle works, and might be used against them. When the King's troops came up they found both these churches down, and their sites bare. The material had gone to strengthen the defences.
2 Matthew Paris, in his 'Chronica Majora,' refers to the destruction of St. Paul's, and Ralf of Coggeshall mentions that of St. Cuthbert's. The act was bitterly resented by the religious, and no doubt by the hapless townsfolk. Paris tells us how the abbess of Elstow, hearing of the outrage, removed the sword from the hand of a statue of St. Paul, until such time as the insult should be avenged.

---

1. Clark. Med. Mil. Arch. I. p. 219.
2. M. Paris. C. M. p. 87; Cog. Chron. p. 205.

In one matter, the main passages of the drama are like the play with a missing hero, for Fawkes de Breauté was not with the garrison now shut up within the castle. The Dunstable Chronicle says: "In the meanwhile, Falcasius withdrew himself, hanging about on the land of the Earl of Chester. But the same Earl, and the Bishop of Winchester, and the Earl of Albemarle," and others, "with their satellites, followed the army of the King, but in mere pretence, and by all their words and works brought themselves under suspicion. At length, indeed, when the Bishop of Winchester and the Earl of Chester saw that they were shut out from the private counsels of the King, they turned aside to their own places."[1] So Fawkes made himself busy outside, doing his best, but vainly, to raise a fresh rebellion, much sought after by the King's men, but not to be taken. Part of the time he was with his associate the Earl of Chester, and once he rushed across to the Welsh hills that he might confer with Llewelyn; whereof we shall hear anon in the Royal Letters. Meanwhile, his brother William watched from his battlements for his coming, just as Stoessel at Port Arthur watched for the relieving armies of Kuropatkin.

vii. Concerning the Siege Artillery.

Now were such of the Bedford folk as remained in the town, but outside the zone of danger, to become witnesses of a full-dress siege, conducted with all the science and skill of the times. It must have been a picturesque business, and yet big with the issues of life and death. Over and above the King's staff, with his barons, knights, and common soldiers, there was a great concourse of bishops and clergy, abbots and monks, with Stephen, the Archbishop, at their head.

---

1. Duns. Chron. p. 87.

On three successive days, the King's officers, with whom was the prior of Newenham, formally demanded the surrender of the castle, and the release of the captured justice. William de Breauté returned a defiant refusal. His brother was rightful lord of the castle, he said, and owned no allegiance to the King; an answer more to be understood in France than in England. Whereupon the King swore, " by the soul of his father " John, that when
1 the castle was taken, he would hang them all. A fairly full-sized oath for a youth of 16.

The clergy now make the next move. There was a stately religious procession and solemn function, when, with candles lighted, the good Archbishop launched the ban of excommunication against Falcasius de Breauté, and all who were holding the
2 castle for him. This was on Thursday, the 20th of June. Next day, the King and Hubert de Burgh arrived, and the pageantry of war was in full flower. The old town has never seen the like, either before or since.

In these early days, the King's soldiers and craftsmen were toiling hard to build and set up their larger siege artillery. There were solid platforms to be made to receive it, earth and timber ramparts to be reared to protect it.

The engines must be posted beyond cross-bow range, and the Dunstable men had told their prior where they remembered seeing the chief of them at work. On the east was the biggest stone-slinger they had, a great petrary, and also two mangonells, which assailed the keep on the mound. On the west, beyond the site of St. Paul's, were two more mangonells to batter the " ancient tower," which gives us a clue as to its position. It probably stood on the western wall of the inner bailey, and was perhaps the gate-tower between the two baileys. On the south,
3 across the river, was another mangonell, and on the north, per-

1. M. Paris. H. A. p. 263; C. M. p. 86.
2. Ibid. C. M. pp. 85 and 88.
3. Duns. Chron. p. 87.

haps near St Peter's green, yet another. Besides these, there were no doubt many other catapults of sorts, and the big bolt-hurling balistæ.

It will be of interest to understand the nature and service of the various machines.

The Mangonell was a catapult on the skip-jack principle. Between two upright posts were strained strands of twisted cord, or preferably horsehair or sinew, and the butt-end of the beam was caught into these. It was drawn down by windlass and rope until horizontal; the stone, say 50lbs. in weight, was lodged in the spoon-shaped hollow at the other end of the beam, or in the sling, when it had one, as in the case of those used in this siege; and, when released by pulling the catch, would fling its missile 350 to 400 yards.

The Balista was a mighty bow which shot heavy shafts 4 to 6 feet long, winged with leather. It was deadly direct for a range of 400 to 500 yards. The bow was framed of a pair of planks held centrally in upright twists of cord or horsehair. The rope or bow-string from the ends was also wound back by windlass, and then let fly. It was, in fact, a giant cross-bow, from which the smaller weapon is believed to have been evolved.

The Petrary was undoubtedly a 'trebuchet,' an instrument only now making its way into general use, and much the most powerful engine of the times. Its beam was laid like that of the mangonell, the butt end projecting beyond the frame-work, and loaded with enormous weights in a sort of iron-ribbed basket. It needed a strong crew to windlass it down, and when released the counterpoise fell and brought the beam back to the upright with immense force. Sir R. Payne-Gallway found that a weight of 20,000 lbs., with a beam of 50 feet, would cast a stone of 300 lbs. [1]
300 yards. The aim was more direct than that of the mangonell, and its service more certain.

---

1. For full description of these engines, with illustrations, see Payne-Gallwey's "Crossbow"; also Viollet le Duc. p. 36.

In all these engines, pads of leather deadened the impact of the swinging beam, and lessened the shock to the framework. The merry men who handled these various engines, in the sieges of the day, used to have nick-names for them, just as our soldiers at Ladysmith called a Boer gun " Long Tom," or one of their own " Joe Chamberlain." Amongst these old nick-names occur such sportive designations as "War-wolf," "Wild-cat," and "Malvoisin" or " Bad neighbour."

viii. Concerning the Assaults.

The summer days were long, but not long enough for the work in hand. When once issue was joined, attack and defence went on day and night.

The Dunstable Annals give us the order in which the main
1 assaults were made. On the barbican with its projecting fore-work facing St. Paul's, fell the first fury of the assault. Apparently, it was only weakly held. Its parapets and timber brattices battered by mangonell stones, its denuded wall-tops searched by the bolts of balistæ and cross-bows, at last came the rush of men-at-arms, who would take no denial. The Chronicle tells us that four or five 'forinseci' fell in its capture, de Breauté's foreign adventurers, who were the backbone of his strength. Then the royal forces secured the hold they had gained, and made ready for further efforts. After each hubbub of assault comes a temporary lull, but always the great stone shot are flying with their long, lazy sweep, the big bolts of the balistæ in a straighter course, and the little whizzing shafts of the cross-bows.

Up in St. Mary's tower, at eventide, we may picture soldiers and citizens climbing to overlook the scene, and to listen to the voices of the instruments in the deadly orchestra of the siege.

---

1. Duns. Chron. p. 87.

Perhaps even a venturesome maid may mount with her squire to receive interesting lessons in the art of war.

" Hark to the snapping of the arblasts!" he whispers. " That dull ' whang ' is the springing of a balista ; and the bolt has sped true" ; his word being justified by a shout of pain from the walls. " That bang of wood against wood means that the mangonells are being loosed ; and that last clash and rattle is the voice of the petrary." A moment later there is a thud, the bellow of cattle, and the scurry of stampeding hoofs. The squire explains that the stone has fallen amongst the beasts in the outer bailey.

As the dusk deepens and vision fails, sounds become more penetrating and ominous ; the smash of stone shot against walls, the rumbling fall of parapets or turrets, the shouts of rage and derision, and, through all, the rustle of unresting movement.

Then the young soldier points to a tall structure of timber ribs and cross-pieces which lifts its black scaffold lines high up against the evening sky to the eastward. On it creep small, dark figures, in silhouette, and the sharp "rabadab" of hammering swings over on the wind, now louder, now fainter. " There is one of our beffrois! Look out for that! It has to go up twice as high yet, before its top can oversee the parapet of the keep. When it does, the end will be at hand. Now, I must away to my post. To-morrow we have business on foot. To-morrow we shall wake new echoes in your sleepy borough." So they [1] descend from their outlook.

To-morrow comes, and, of a sudden, new roar of battle breaks out ; this time, within the castle. For the mangonells by St. Peter's and across the river have breached the thinner walls of the outer bailey facing them, and thus the way is open on both [2] sides at once. Why not also from the captured barbican? Because it was a mere approach to the main gate, and we have

---

1. Imaginary, but founded on the actualities of the case.

2. Duns. Chron. p. 87.

no word of that having been forced. Portcullis, drawbridge, and flanking towers, no doubt, made it so strong that it was easier to turn it by breaching the lateral walls. The townsmen listen and wonder. The cattle low, the pigs shriek, and the hoarse yells of men in strife rises above the clang and rattle of arms.

Dunstable lads are in it. "Many were slain in that scrimmage," they report, "but we came out of it well, for we gat much plunder; horses and harness, chain mail loricæ and balistæ, 'boves et bacones et porcos vivos,' more than we could count up.
1 And we set their sheds alight for them, full of corn and fodder."

As the storm dies down, men rush out with the news of their success, flushed and red-eyed with the fury of battle; and now and then, others straggle through, more sober slow, bound up with red bandages. For they who thrust hand into rat-hole must look to be bitten, even though the rat come to grief in the end. Word flies that the whole outer bailey is taken, with all its stores. There now only remain to the garrison the inner bailey, with its "old tower," and the great mounded keep, but the stiffest part of the work is still to come.

There is no long respite, for probably the actual fighting in the four assaults, as described by the Dunstable Chronicle, occurred after weeks of preparation and bombardment. The miners from the Forest of Dean get to work, and go burrowing into the great ramparts under the inner bailey walls. What are the besieged about to let them in under, so long as they have stones to hurl, or cross-bows for sharp-shooting? The reason is that the sappers are working under cover. For while some of the King's carpenters were hammering away at their 'berefrida' or 'beffrois,' others were busily shaping another machine;
2 'testudo,' Matthew Paris calls it, the Dunstable men, more colloquially, the 'cat.'

---

1. Ibid. 43. M. Paris. C. M. p. 85.
2. M. Paris. C. M. p. 86.; Duns. Chron. p. 87.

Now the 'cat' is a famous animal in the sieges of the day. It was a strong shed on wheels, like an overgrown bathing-machine, sometimes iron-clad as to its sloping roof, to be thrust close up to defending walls, that the 'mineatores' may dig and delve under cover, cutting their 'cuniculi,' coney-shafts, well into the stuff below the foundations.

An old French poem, describing the siege of Boves by Philip Augustus, in 1205, thus speaks of the cat:—

"They cause a cat to be drawn on the bridge;
The miners throw themselves beneath;
The strong wall they begin to mine;
And make the cat so shelter them 1
That naught can them embarrass."

Cats were sometimes foiled by having their roofs battered in by the big stone shot. A few years before, Simon de Montfort, had one of his cats broken up thus, when besieging an Albigen-
sian town. "Par Dieu!" cried the bystanders, "Dame Cat will 2
never catch the rats."

The royal cat, so busy with the banks and walls of the inner bailey, was a more successful beast. The masonry comes tumbling down, and a breach was opened near the 'old tower' in the west wall facing St. Paul's. Matters were now ripe for the third assault. The Dunstable men were again in the thick of it.

"Entering by the gap," says the Chronicler, "our men took possession of the inner bailey; a very dangerous business, and many of them lost their lives." Ten of them even made a rush to get into the keep itself, but that was more than they could
manage, and they were promptly snapped up by the enemy and 3
laid by the heels inside.

1. Guiart, from Viollet le Duc. p. 35.
2. Viollet le Duc. p. 34.
3. Duns. Chron, p. 88.

Again there was a brief respite. Things were now looking black for the garrison. Fawkes de Breauté's banner still flies on on the keep, but all else is lost. The lanky timber-legs of the
1 two 'berefrida,' "fabricatum architectoria arte," says the St. Albans writer, now lift their ungainly length high above the topmost battlements of the keep. Within a protected outlook on the top, the 'collum' or neck, lurk the cross-bowmen, who make it too hot for anything to appear on walls or turrets. No doubt, too, the keep parapets were now broken down by the stone fire, and any timber 'bretasches' knocked to pieces.

Still the rats can bite, for about this time, two of the King's knights were slain by bolts, and many of his men; desperate attack goading the garrison to desperate defence. Matthew Paris names one of the knights, a certain Gifford, "miles elegantis-
2 simus"; and Ralph of Coggeshall tells us that Richard de Argentine, Sheriff of Herts. and Essex, and Governor of Hertford castle, was seriously wounded by a bolt through chain mail and body. Also that six stout knights were killed, and of those "who worked about the engines, more than 200, so they say."

Whilst the wall-fighters of the keep are cowed by the fire from the 'beffrois,' another 'cat' is pushing hard up against the mound and keep foot. Although petrary and mangonells have been banging away incessantly, it is clear that even after 9 weeks of bombardment, no vital damage has been done to the main structure, or this mining work would not have been
3 necessary. Both from Dunstable and St. Albans we learn the main facts of the final blow. "Not without much hurt to many," says the latter, were the cats thrust into position. Through earth of mound, and foundations of keep, the 'mineatores' dig

1. M. Paris. C. M. p. 86; Duns. Chron. p. 87.
2. M. Paris. C. M. p. 85; Cog. Chron. p. 206.
3. Duns. Chron. p. 88; M. Paris. C. M. p. 86; Cog. Chron. p. 207.

their galleries, as they go, propping up the wall with balks of timber, that the super-structure may not come down on their heads. When all is ready they pile up combustibles about the timber, and then retire.

It is late in the afternoon of the 14th August, the "eve of the
Assumption of the Blessed Mary." Eager watchers from the 1
beffrois, from St. Mary's tower, and from the nearer works of the besiegers, at first see only a little curl of smoke making its way out, where the now empty cat abuts against the mound and wall. It grows denser and pours out in volume. Loud cracks are heard, and the smoke begins to issue from within the keep itself. Then, under their eyes, a section of the wall slowly subsides, falling away with a crash, and rumbling down on to cat and mound. Through the dust cloud which rises, timbers and roofs within are seen to be alight, and defenders are scurrying away in hot haste from the shattered point.

The keep is now defenceless. At any moment the assault may be ordered, and the result cannot be in doubt. There is a long pause, and then the banner of de Breauté begins slowly to flutter down the staff on the keep top, like a butterfly with broken wings; another moment, and another banner is run up, of
red, with the three golden leopards of the King of England. 2
Then a mighty shout rings out from the besieging army, and the delighted townsfolk, as they realise that this is the end, and that the siege is over.

Here it may be noted that two facts in the record of the final scene prove that the keep was of the round 'shell' type, and not one of the great four-square kind. (1) If it had been the latter, as at Norham, or Rochester, with walls of enormous thickness,

---

1. Duns. Chron. p. 88.
2. Ibid., also Heraldic Note by W. H. St. J. H.

it could not have been effectively breached by undermining a small part of it in the way described; and (2) its height, plus that of the mound, would have required beffrois of extraordinary dimensions to out-top it. It must, therefore, have been a round 'shell' keep, a smaller Windsor, in fact, but with walls of no
1 great altitude or thickness. Matthew Paris, in his sketch, confirms this deduction. Once breached, it lay at the mercy of the attackers, and hence the collapse of the defence, on the 14th August.

Now we must draw on all the three Chroniclers, and weave their various strands into one, without always waiting to acknowledge our debt.

As the King's banner crowns the fissured keep, a little party of men and women makes its way out in the direction of the royal headquarters. As they come near they prove to be the captive-
2 in-chief, Henry de Braibroc, Margaret, the wife of Fawkes de Breauté, the other women who were shut up with her, and the captured soldiers of the King's army. Amongst them, let us hope, the unlucky, over plucky, ten men from Dunstable. They were led before the King and the Justiciar.

Henry de Braibroc, overjoyed to find himself free and safe,
3 gave thanks to God, St. Leonard, and the King, for his deliverance. In truth, his escape was a narrow one, for towards the last, some of the garrison had made a rush to cut his throat, whilst others urged in favour of making their submission. It was well for them that they held their hand, as, but for the presence of the prisoners, the King was minded to have let none out of the keep,
4 and to have burnt them all where they stood.

That night the King's troops kept guard over the garrison, now prisoners themselves. Next morning, William de Breauté, his

---

1. See Frontispiece.
2. Duns. Chron. p. 88.
3. M. Paris. H. A. p. 265.
4. Ibid. p. 264.

knights and retainers, were first released from excommunication, shriven, and then solemnly hung on rough gallows under the shadow of the keep. Fawkes himself, not being present, had all his possessions confiscated to pay the heavy expenses of the siege, and was still held excommunicate until he had delivered
over two castles still held by him, Plympton and Stokes Curci. 1
Already the King had impounded money and jewels which William Martel, brother of Fawkes, had lodged with the Priory of
St. Neots, as noted in the Close Roll. Plympton castle had been 2
the subject of a letter from de Breauté to the Justiciar, so far back as March, 1221. He complains that the Devonshire people are giving him trouble, and that Robert de Courtenay will not let him
provision the castle. This stronghold had belonged to William 3
de Ripariis or Redvers. His son Baldwin, Earl of Albemarle, was de Breaute's wife's first husband, who died leaving her with a son. On her second marriage with Fawkes, Plympton was her dower, together with other large possessions.

Now the poor lady, when released from the annoyances of the Bedford siege, makes a startling statement to the King and his Council. She had never wanted Fawkes to husband; far from it. He had taken advantage of the unsettled times, had pounced upon her, carried her off, and made her wed him against
her will. "Now," said she, "I want my divorce." The result 4
is not stated, but after a day or two of deliberation all her lands and possessions throughout England were restored to her, and she was placed under wardship to William, Count de Warenne.

All the survivors of the castle garrison had been hanged, save only the chaplain, who was handed over to the Archbishop, to be dealt with according to Canon law, Roger Wendover gives

1. Duns. Chron. p. 89.
2. Patent Roll. p. 448, also M. Paris. C. M. p. 85.
3. Royal Letters. CXLIX. p. 172.
4. M. Paris. C. M. p. 87.

the number at "about 24," Matthew Paris adds on the margin,
1 when retelling the story, "double the number"; Dunstable says
"eighty and more"; Ralph of Coggeshall, 83.

The King's vow was kept. He hanged them all. Yet three survived their hanging. They were Knights Templar, who had seen service in the Holy Land. They were strung up with the rest, for the soul of a John was a solemn thing to swear by. As
2 soon, however, as they were fairly a-dangle, the King had them
cut down again, and they came back to earth, no doubt, somewhat astonished at their rare experience. Their comrades were less lucky, and continued to hang. This is the true end of the drama, and Matthew Paris thought so, for he made a nice little drawing on his margin of some of them on their gallows of tree trunks,
3 with de Breauté's banner over them, and the keep above all, with
the King's banner flying from its summit.

Matthew does not fail to rub the obvious moral in, both by word and drawing, and he tells how the popular verdict fell into a jingling couplet.

4 "Perdidit in mense, Falco tam fervidus ense,
Omine sub sævo, quicquid quæsivit ab ævo."

which may be freely paraphrased in English:—

When fortune frowned,
Success disowned
Falco of the fiery sword;
In one short moon
Was gone so soon,
Falco's long amasséd hoard.

As a matter of fact, the siege lasted almost nine weeks; from Thursday, 20th June, the day of the third summons and excommunication, to Wednesday, 14th August.

---

1. M. Paris. C. M. p. 87; Duns. Chron. p. 88; Cog. Chron. p. 207.
2. Duns. Chron. p. 88; M. Paris. H A. p. 264.
3. See Frontispiece.
3. M. Paris. H. A. p. 266 and C. M. p. 87. See Text, top line of Frontispiece.

ix. Concerning the after fortunes of Fawkes de Breaute.

Nothing now remains but to follow the closing scenes of Fawkes de Breauté's career.

One of the Royal Letters confirms the statement that during the siege, he had been with his friend the Earl of Chester. Early in August the Earl writes to the King, "I know well why you have turned aside to besiege Bedford Castle, and in what manner Falcasius de Breauté has answered. But when it has seemed good to you to notify to me concerning the lord Falcasius that by means of his men, as you have heard, he was contriving to do you evil, 'pro certo,' be it known to you that this I have never known, nor been able to understand. Verily, I have well seen and understood that he is very sad and sorry about your wrath, always, since you have been angry and provoked against him, bearing himself patiently, and free of any offence towards you, especially as to leading enemies on to your land, inasmuch as he has always desired and does desire, if it may please you, to recover your favour by the help of friends, and to be able to placate your aforesaid anger towards him." 1

The Earl then goes on to say that he is glad to serve the King, and that he has got Llewelyn to agree to a month's truce.

Towards the end of July, Llewelyn himself had written a very spirited letter to the King. "To his reverend lord and dearest brother Henry, by the Grace of God King of England, lord of Ireland, duke of Normandy and Aquitania, count of Andegavia,—Llewelyn, Prince of North Wales, with dutiful affection, greeting." He refers to the siege of "the said Falcasius, his castle," and then proceeds: "Also you have forbidden us (royal us), to give him either help or counsel, or to receive either himself or his people. To this we answer you that the said

1. Royal Letters. CCIV. p. 233.

Falcasius came to us in our own country, complaining and grieving heavily over the things which your Council had caused to be done to him. He showed also that he was no party to, nor aware of the capture of the said Henry (de Braibroc), and certainly he should not defend the deed. The rather he proposed that he should cause William de Breauté and his followers to stand their trial, and give satisfaction. But, whereas he denies to your Council that he had acted unjustly, as to that he was content to explain. On the same day on which he came to us he departed from our country. We would impress this upon you. That we are not to be taken as excusing ourselves if we receive him and his men. For, certainly we have not less liberty than the King of Scotland, who receives outlaws from England, and that unchallenged. Moreover, the aforesaid Falcasius had in no way behaved ill towards you, nor towards your father, of blessed memory,"

He continues that he had never heard Fawkes speak evil of Henry, but rather much good, and that he desired above all to serve the King in all things. There is much more of the same frank and independent tone.

"Besides this, you have made known to us that the said Falcasius is under sentence as a disturber of the realm. But, 'pro certo,' you should know that they are rather the disturbers of the realm who proffer counsel to you of small value, so that you have thrust out great men, and men necessary to you, from your presence and Council, disinheriting them, and oppressing them without cause, through sheer self-will. If, thus violently bereft of his possessions, the said Falcasius stands on his defence against the lord Pope, we do not believe he would be excommunicate before God. Whatsoever, indeed, others may do, concerning these matters, or anything else, we will do nothing against our own conscience. For, indeed, we would choose rather to be excommunicated by man, than to do anything contrary to God, our own conscience condemning us. Both in these things, and others,

may God grant wholesome counsel to you and to us, because we
stand in much need thereof.—Farewell." 1

Bravo! Llewelyn! But we much doubt whether the young whippersnapper of a King, with his ingenious methods of doing reverence to his late father's soul, will have soul enough himself to appreciate you. In any case, it is refreshing, after having looked at "the aforesaid Falcasius" through the spectacles of king, constable and monk, to find that there may have been something to say on his side, and to hear it said so well and bravely. On August 12, two days before the keep fell, the King issues letters of safe-conduct for Fawkes, to all "Sheriffs, bailiffs, and faithful subjects." To wit—that the venerable father, Stephen, Archbishop, with certain of his bishops, is to meet Fawkes de Breauté at Northampton, with those of his household, now excommunicate, that they may there receive absolution; and that they were all to have safe-conduct as far as that town, within a certain specified time; and that none were to molest them, or do
them injury. 2

Matthew Paris gives us a detailed account of de Breauté's arrival at Bedford and meeting with the King, when he had been
brought down from Northampton; all of which the Annalist 3
received first-hand from Alexander Stavenby, Bishop of Coventry, who had the prisoner under his charge.

When the broken man saw his brother and near friends hanging on their gibbet, he fell to the ground in a fit. When he came to himself, breathing heavily, he burst out into penitent ejaculations. "Truly hath St. Alban, against whom I offended, stricken me down with his great stone!" Then, when led into the King's presence, he spake much of his past services, and begged for mercy.

---

1. Royal Letters. CCI. p. 229.
2. Ibid. CCV. p. 235, from Patent Roll.
3. M. Paris. A. H. p. 265 and C. M. p. 87.

The reference to the "great stone" needs explanation.
In former days, some time after the famous raid,
Pandulf, the Papal Legate, the Bishop-elect of Norwich, once
chanced to meet de Breauté, and thus accosted him: "Have you
ever, in any way, offended St. Alban? For I saw in a vision a
1 great assembly in his church, and you were there. And, lo! of
a sudden a mighty stone fell from a tower on your head, and when
2 I looked again, you were not." Skilful dreamer, and apt
interpretation!

From Bedford, de Breauté was taken to London by Eustace
de Falconberg, bishop of that city; who, on receiving him, said
with a laugh, "You have destroyed the church of St Paul, and
3 here his minister has you in custody." Meanwhile, the Elstow
abbess restored to the statue of St. Paul the sword she had taken
away.

From London, de Breauté, now condemned to exile, was
put on board ship for France. King Louis promptly seized him,
4 and, having a good memory of many grievances, was much set on
hanging him. At last, however, the King allowed him to proceed
to Rome, where he badgered the Pope, who in turn badgered boy
Henry, to the end that Fawkes should again be restored to
favour; but all in vain, whereof the matter may be read in sundry
letters which have survived.

In fact, the Pope had already acted on his behalf.
He had written at length, on 17th August, to the Archbishop at Bedford, laying injunctions on him to revoke the excommunication, and to prevent any attack on de Breauté. At the
5 same date he also wrote the King, bidding him desist from the
siege. As the castle was taken three days before these long
letters were written, they naturally fell somewhat flat.

---

1. See Plate III.
2. M. Paris. C. M. p. 120.
3. Ibid. A. H. p. 265.
4. Ibid. C. M. pp. 94 and 97.
5. Royal Letters. Appendix Nos. 19 and 20. p. 544.

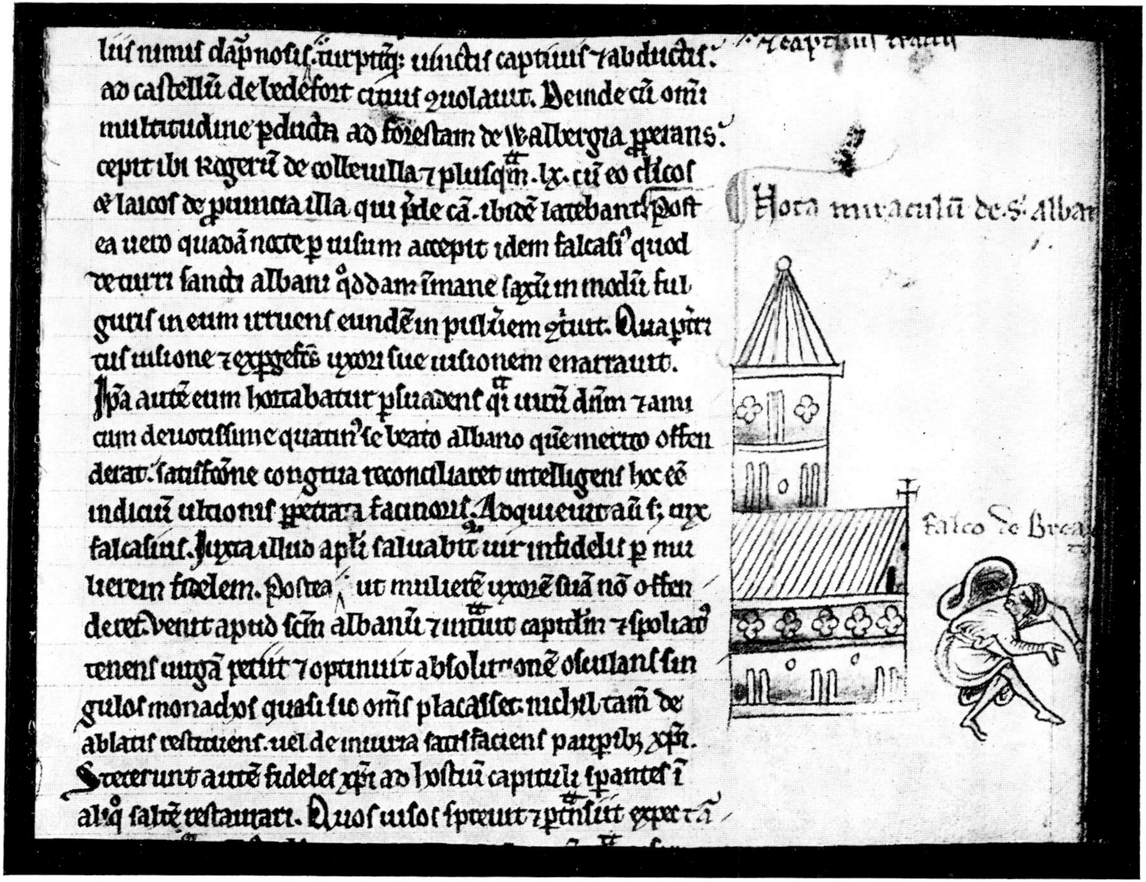

Plate III.

The Great Stone falling on Fawkes de Breauté at St. Albans.

Matthew Paris. 'Chronica Majora.' Vol. III. fol. 50.

For two years the agitation over de Breauté was kept alive.
In 1226, as he went to and fro on the business, he chanced to stay
at the French town of St Ciriac. There, one night after eating
fish at supper, he retired to rest, and was found dead in bed. The
fish are stated to have been poisoned. " Black and corrupting,"
remarks Matthew Paris, " intestate and unshrived, and empty of
all honour, he was quickly buried in an ignoble grave; and thus
1 horribly ended his evil life, receiving the fruit of his works, and
to be mourned with dry tears." The artist scribe adds, in his
2 upper margin, a sketch of a demon despatching a fish into de
Breauté's mouth. It would have been interesting to have heard
Llewelyn's comment on the above remarks. He had good reason
to know something of Fawkes de Breauté, as he had married his
3 daughter Eva for his second wife.

One good wish Matthew Paris does give expression to.
" Would that that stone (St. Alban's stone), only many times more
4 terrible, may not now be pounding him to pieces in hell!"

We have seen that, during the siege, the King had impounded money and valuables deposited by the rebels with certain monastic houses. After his death, a much larger amount comes into question. There is a Royal Letter to Robert de Shardelaw, or Sherlaw, apparently one of the officers of the Temple, in London, which deals with the matter. When his affairs had become desperate, Fawkes de Breauté, had lodged a sum of 11,000 marks, or £7,333 6s. 8d., " in domo Templi Ierosolymitani." The King explains that, during his minority, de Breauté, as his Sheriff of seven counties, had turned this money, and much more besides, to his own purposes, instead of paying it into the Royal Exchequer, and that when his castle was taken and he sought the King's mercy, he had handed over the

1. M. Paris. C. M. p. 121.
2. See Plate IV.
3. Dict. Nat. Biog. VI. p. 251.
4. M. Paris. C. M. p. 121.

PLATE IV.

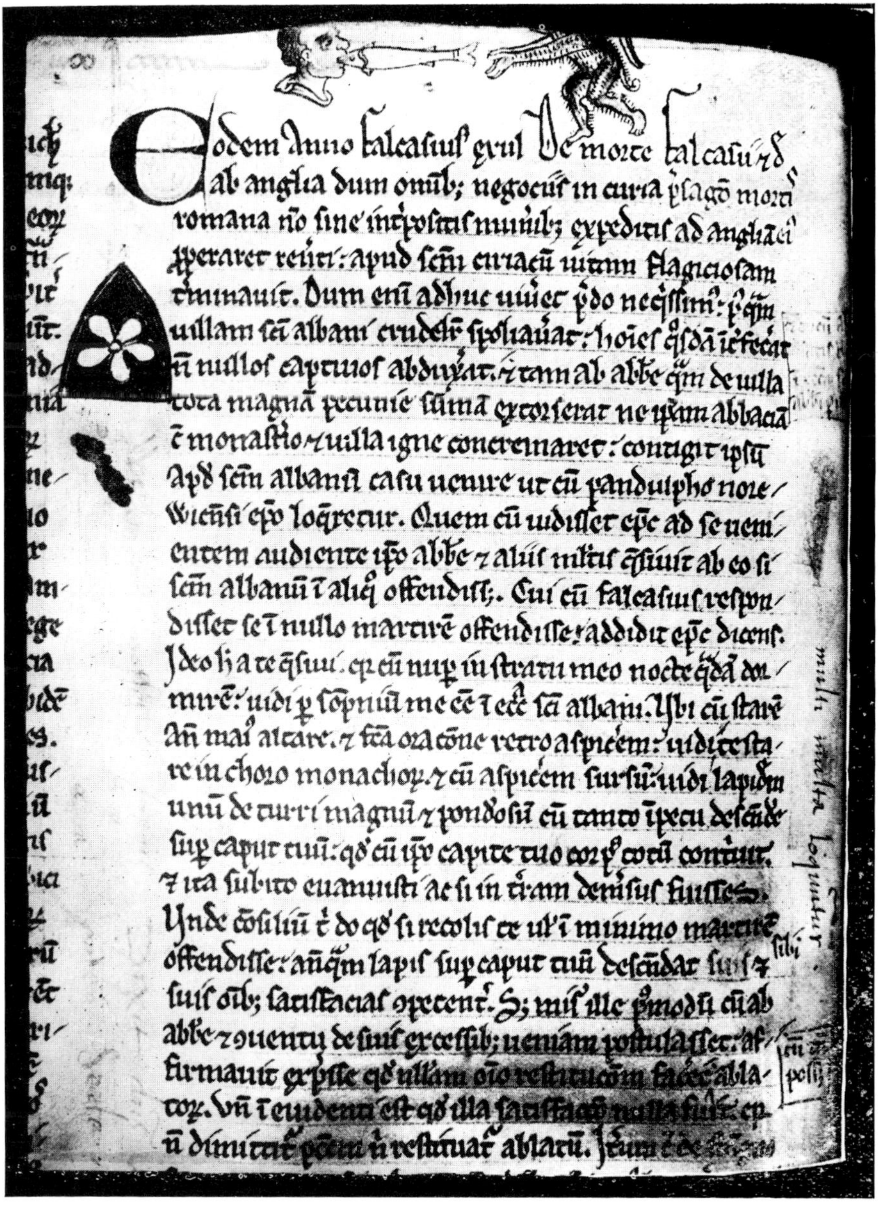

DE BREAUTÉ'S DEATH.

Matthew Paris 'Chronica Majora'
Vol. III. fol. 65, *dorso.*

sum of forty shillings, declaring on his oath that it was all he possessed. "In which, clearly, he had committed the crime of perjury, when he had nothing divulged to us concerning this money, set down at 11,000 marks." The King states that he had written the Pope begging him to order its restitution, and that he wants Robert de Sherlaw to use his influence both with the Pope, and the "brothers" of the order, to the same end. For the Master of the Temple, "in our land of England," could be made to hand the money over, but the King chose rather to move the Pope to an act of justice than to carry the matter with a high
1 hand. The letter is dated from Windsor, 12 September, 1227.

x. Concerning the Destruction of the Castle.

As for the castle, its story was now at an end. Strict orders were issued for its destruction. The Dunstable writer, with accuracy, tells us that the Sheriff was ordered to demolish the keep and outer
2 bailey, while the inner bailey, dismantled, and its fosse everywhere levelled up, was given to William de Beauchamp for his occupation. Both in the Close Rolls and Royal Letters very definite details appear as to this destruction, and William de Beauchamp's disgust thereat. Not thus had he looked to receive his ancestral stronghold. The item in the Close Rolls has almost a flavour of satire in it. After ordering the demolition of the keep and outer-bailey, it proceeds: "But the walls of the lesser bailey are to be reduced to one-half their height, and to remain without parapets; which walls it is permitted to our dear and faithful William de Beauchamp to put a coping on, and if he likes to build for himself a mansion within them. Three-quarters of the old tower towards St. Paul's are to be levelled with the

---

1. Royal Letters. CCLVII. p. 313.
2. Duns. Chron. p. 88; M. Paris. C. M. p. 87.

ground." This order was given under the King's hand at Bedford 1
on 20 August, six days after the surrender.

In a letter of the next day, a writer, supposed to be the Archdeacon of Bedford, reports that "the faithful William," takes the matter very ill. "He begins to be cantankerous against the order of the Lord King as to the destruction of the castle." He wants to do what he likes with the stone. He does not want the "pavements in the ditches" to be destroyed. So the writer prays urgently that the lord King should be asked to write very 2
straitly if he wishes his original orders to be carried out.

On the 25 August the lord King does so write from London again to the Sheriff. The instructions as to the lesser bailey are to be executed as given. But when the 'mota,' the mound, shall have been reduced as ordered, then William de Beauchamp may enclose the site of it with a wall, namely, of the same height with 3
the wall of the inner bailey, when reduced.

These references are of value in helping us to place the various works of the castle. Some have taken the old tower to have stood on the outermost wall near St. Paul's. But it was clearly part of the inner bailey on that side. And the curious order that three-quarters of it are to be destroyed "down to the ground," evidently means that it was to be gutted, and only its external wall left to continue the line of the inner bailey wall. Also the keep was close to that bailey, for the mound on which it stood might be included within practically the same wall.

The demolition was thoroughly carried out. The stone from the ruins was, part of it, handed over to the canons of St. Paul's for the re-building of the church, and part to Newenham Priory. 4
The detail of the earliest work in St. Paul's agrees with this period of its rebuilding.

---

1. Close Rolls. p. 632 and Beds. Arch. Trans., XII., p. 249.
2. Royal Letters. CCVI. p. 236.
3. Beds. Arch. Trans., XII., p. 249. for item from Close Roll.
4. Duns. Chron. p. 88. Part of the stone also went to Caldwell Priory.

The after history of the place is obscure. Business and pleasure—breweries, shop premises, and gardens—have, on the townward sides of the site, wiped out all the lines of such remains as survived the destruction. The river, mighty in its floods, century after century, has no doubt made level plain of as much
1 of the old earthworks as it could lap away on the south. Traces of the outermost enclosing ditch have been found in Ram Yard, on the north, by the Swan Inn, at the south-west angle, and
2 bounding Mr. Higgin's garden on the east. Only the stump of the great moated mound remains, with a short section of its surrounding fosse.

The present surface of the mound has long been famous as one of the oldest bowling greens in England. Leland, Camden, De Foe, and Lysons, all refer to it. Mr. Higgins may suitably show it to our American cousins as an illustration why our English turf is so superfine. "How on earth do you manage it?" enquired one of them. "Nothing easier," said a gardener. "Mow it, and roll it, for two or three hundred years,—and there you are!" If he had stood on the Bedford mound, he might have said "four hundred."

1. Wyatt. Beds. Arch. Trans., IX., p. 281.
2. See Plate II.